ANOTHER NEWFOUNDLAND SCOFF

A PICTORIAL COOKBOOK

DALE WILSON
FLANKER PRESS

For Julie, with love.

A Flanker Press Book

Published by Flanker Press Ltd., 2003
St. John's, Newfoundland and Labrador

Flanker Press Ltd.
PO Box 2522, Stn. C
St. John's, NL
A1C 6K1

National Library of Canada Cataloguing in Publication Data
Wilson, Dale, 1958-
Another Newfoundland Scoff: a pictorial cookbook / Dale Wilson
ISBN 1-894463-34-X
1. Cookery—Newfoundland. 2. Cookery, Canadian—Maritime style. I. Title.
TX715.6.W547854 2003   641.59718   C2003-900679-4

PHOTOGRAPHY   Dale Wilson
FOOD STYLING   Debbie Arthurs Page
BOOK DESIGN   Trivium Design Inc.
PRINTING   Friesens

Printed and Bound in Canada

Scoff *noun* [associated with food]: usually a meal served in the evening as part of a party; often prepared with (stolen) ingredients from a neighbour's garden—such as cabbage for a Jiggs Dinner.

INTRODUCTION

My father-in-law always greets me at the door with a resounding "Welcome home." Invariably the kettle will have been heated and a cup of tea turns into an all-out meal. Undoubtedly Nan will look at me strangely when I finally say "enough." How could she possibly be insulted? I have obligingly and very willingly devoured the long-awaited—and second-to-none—homemade bread, as well as having sampled the various other offerings that just moments before had filled the table to overflowing capacity.

Such is the homecoming when I venture to the small Burin Peninsula community of Lewin's Cove. I am also made to feel right at home with the many friends I have made over my years of travelling the length and breadth of this province. So, too, have the many CFA's (Come-From-Away's) who have embraced all this land and its people have to offer.

Just as the dialects of its early European descendants pay homage to their Irish, French and English ancestry, the landscape is equally contagious. Rugged granite coastlines reach heavenward like fingers from the sea; deep-cut inland fjords slice apart millennia-old mountains like a butcher's cleaver; the bump-and-grind of plate tectonics have exposed the earth's very core as a nakedness not seen elsewhere on this planet.

Whereas the geology is rugged and hearty, so too are her people; the two fit together like a pocket on a shirt. These are the people who have historically foraged a living from the bounty of the land and sea. It is hard work, and the traditional food of the island—and mainland Labrador—is befitting the recipients: solid, heavy and unpretentious. Lace and pastries are reserved for society.

This is a slice of Canada where one's very senses are tantalized, teased and cajoled to inhuman proportions—a delectable scoff.

Dale Wilson
February 2003

CONTENTS

BACON-WRAPPED SCALLOPS

1 LB		**whole scallops**
½ LB		**bacon**
1 TBSP		**garlic salt**

Preparation Time
15 minutes

Broiling Time
6-8 minutes

Makes 4 servings

1. Preheat broiler.
2. Rinse scallops.
3. Wrap each scallop with ½ bacon strip. If scallops are small then bacon can be cut in half lengthwise.
4. Secure with toothpick and place in shallow baking pan.
5. Sprinkle with garlic salt and broil for 6-8 minutes until scallops are browned and bacon is crisp.

STEAMED MUSSELS

Preparation Time
10 minutes

Cooking Time
8-10 minutes

Makes 4 servings

4 LBS	mussels, cleaned
¼ CUP	salt
8 CUPS	water
¼ CUP	butter, melted

1. Place mussels, salt and water in a large covered pot.
2. Bring to a boil and steam for 8-10 minutes or until shells open.
3. Drain and cool.
4. Discard any unopened shells.
5. Serve mussels in shell with melted butter, for dipping.

Many of the 15,000-year-old icebergs that pass by the Newfoundland coastline were calved from the glaciers along Greenland's west coast. Of the 40,000 medium- to large-sized icebergs that calve annually, only about 400-800 will survive the trip as far south to Witless Bay.

First named by the French as "Petite"—meaning little or small—Petty Harbour was originally used as a summer fishing station by French, Spanish and Portuguese fishermen. The big-budget movie *Orca*, featuring Bo Derek and Richard Harris, was filmed here in 1977.

STUFFED SQUID

Preparation Time
20 minutes

Parboil
45 minutes

Baking Time
1½ hours

Makes 4 servings

1 LB	squid tubes
3 CUPS	breadcrumbs
2	small onions, diced
½ CUP	butter, melted
1½ TBSP	savory
½ TSP	garlic salt
DASH	pepper

1. Rinse squid tubes and place in large saucepan.
2. Cover with water. Bring to a boil and simmer for 45 minutes.
3. Remove from water. Drain and let cool.
4. Preheat oven to 350°F.
5. Combine breadcrumbs, onions, butter and seasoning. Fill squid tubes with mixture.
6. Place stuffed squid in baking dish and sprinkle with garlic salt. Pour small amount of water in bottom of pan to prevent burning.
7. Cover and bake for 1½ hours. Check occasionally and add water as needed.
8. Cut into rings to serve.

Preparation Time *20-30 minutes*	⅓ CUP	butter	
	¾ CUP	lightly packed brown sugar	
Baking Time *20-25 minutes*	2	eggs	
	¾ CUP	milk	
Makes 12 servings	½ TSP	vanilla	
	2 CUPS	all-purpose flour	
	4 TSP	baking powder	
	½ TSP	salt	
	¾ CUP	partridgeberries	

Topping (optional)

2 TBSP	brown sugar
½ TSP	cinnamon

1. Preheat oven to 375°F.
2. In mixing bowl, cream butter and brown sugar until light and fluffy. Beat in eggs, then milk and vanilla (mixture may curdle).
3. Sift together flour, baking powder and salt. Add to creamed mixture all at once and stir just enough to dampen dry ingredients.
4. Sprinkle 1 TBSP flour over berries and stir to coat (this prevents berries from sinking to bottom of muffin). Add floured berries to mixture and stir gently.
5. Grease 12 large muffin tins and fill just to top with batter.
6. Combine sugar and cinnamon. Sprinkle over batter.
7. Bake for 20-25 minutes.

SUGGESTED SUBSTITUTE: Any fresh or frozen berry can be used with this recipe. However, the sugar content may have to be adjusted to reflect the sweetness of the substituted berry.

PARTRIDGEBERRY MUFFINS

"I'm retired now you know," said Mr. Jim Cooper, "but I still gets up at a quarter-to-four to see what the day will bring." Mr. Cooper, from Old Shop, Trinity Bay, is taking "rounders" from the salt brine and will place them on the flake to dry in the sun, while Mrs. Cooper looks on.

HOMEMADE BREAD

Preparation Time
30 minutes

Rising Time
3 hours

Baking Time
45-50 minutes

Makes 4 loaves

2 PACKS	yeast
1 CUP	lukewarm water
2 TSP	granulated sugar
2 CUPS	scalded milk
1 CUP	water
3 TSP	salt
3 TBSP	sugar
½ CUP	butter
10-12 CUPS	all-purpose flour, sifted

1. Add yeast to lukewarm water in which 2 TSP sugar has been dissolved. Let stand in a warm place for 10 minutes.
2. Scald milk. Add water, salt, sugar and butter. Cool to lukewarm.
3. Stir yeast and add to the lukewarm milk mixture.
4. Add half of the flour and beat until smooth. Gradually add remaining flour, blending in the last of it with your hand.
5. Knead dough for 10 minutes or until smooth.
6. Place in a greased bowl then cover with greased wax paper and a damp tea towel. Let rise in a warm place until doubled in bulk (about 1½ hours).
7. Punch down the dough and shape into loaves. Place in greased pans and let rise until doubled (about 1 hour).
8. Bake at 350°F for 45 to 50 minutes.

PORK BUNS

Preparation Time
15 minutes

Baking Time
20 minutes

Makes 12 large buns

3 CUPS	all-purpose flour
5 TSP	baking powder
¼ CUP	sugar
½ LB	salt pork (diced very small)
1 CUP	cold water
½ CUPS	raisins (optional)
½ CUP	shortening

1. Preheat oven to 375°F.
2. In skillet, fry salt pork until cooked but not crisp.
3. In mixing bowl, combine flour, baking powder, and sugar. Cut in shortening until mixture is crumbly.
4. Mix in water, raisins and salt pork.
5. Press out onto a floured surface. Cut into desired shape.
6. Place on a cookie sheet and bake for 20 minutes or until golden brown.

SUGGESTED SUBSTITUTE: Bacon can be used as a suitable and slightly sweeter alternative to pork.

The Point Amour lighthouse—the tallest in Atlantic Canada—has been standing sentinel over the Labrador Straits for more than 150 years. Archaeology shows the Paleo-Indians inhabited this area of Labrador as long as 9,000 years ago, yet by 3,000 years ago this Maritime Archaic lifestyle had disappeared.

Few seabirds exhibit such grace and regal-like disposition in the air as the Northern Gannet with its 2-metre wingspan. Of the six gannetries in the western Atlantic Ocean, three are found in Newfoundland. The largest, with 6,500 pairs, is at Cape St. Mary's.

TOUTONS

¼ LB	salt pork, diced
	bread dough for one loaf of bread
	molasses, warmed

Preparation Time
5 minutes

Cooking Time
5-7 minutes

Makes 4 servings

1. Fry salt pork until brown and crisp.
2. Remove pork scraps.
3. Break off small pieces of dough the size of an egg. Flatten in palms of hand until ½ inch thick.
4. Fry dough in pork fat until browned on both sides.
5. Top with warmed molasses.

SUGGESTED SUBSTITUTE: As an alternative the toutons can be fried in vegetable oil instead of salt pork drippings. Pancake syrup or maple syrup makes a nice substitute to molasses.

½ LB	fresh haddock or cod, cubed
½ LB	fresh scallops
½ LB	fresh or frozen shrimp
2 CUPS	cooked lobster meat, cubed
4 TBSP	oil
¼ CUP	celery, diced
1	medium onion, diced
2	medium potatoes, diced
¼ TSP	thyme
2 CUPS	boiling water
1	chicken bouillon cube
1 TSP	salt
1 CUP	blend cream
1 CUP	milk

Preparation Time
30 minutes

Cooking Time
30 minutes

Makes 4-6 servings

1. In a skillet, sauté onion and celery in 2 TBSP oil until soft. Do not brown.
2. Using a second skillet, cover and fry haddock, scallops and shrimp in 2 TBSP oil until cooked, about 10 minutes.
3. In a large pot, boil water and stir in bouillon cube until dissolved.
4. Add potatoes, salt and thyme. Boil until potatoes are tender. Do not drain.
5. Add seafood, onion and celery to the pot. Simmer for 10 minutes.
6. Add cream and milk. Heat gently but do not boil.

The quintessential fishing community of Newfoundland and Labrador, Salvage is located at the tip of the Eastport Peninsula. Narrow turning roads meander throughout the village passing by clapboard houses and freshly painted stores (fish sheds) suggesting automobile traffic and urban engineers were unheard of when settled in 1868.

16

FRESH MEAT SOUP

Preparation Time
30 minutes

Cooking Time
2½-3 hours

Makes 6 servings

1	large beef soup bone with meat
6 CUPS	water
1½ TSP	salt
½ CUP	barley
2	onions, diced
3	carrots, diced
1	medium turnip, diced
1	small cabbage, diced
	pepper to taste

1. Place soup bone, water and salt in a large soup pot. Bring to a boil.
2. Lower heat and simmer 1 hour.
3. Remove soup bone from pot and cut meat into small pieces.
4. Return meat and bone to pot.
5. Add barley and continue to simmer for another hour, stirring often.
6. Add vegetables and continue to cook until meat is very tender.

SUGGESTED SUBSTITUTE: Rice makes a nice alternative to barley.

PEA SOUP AND DUMPLINGS

Preparation Time
30 minutes

Soaking Time
Overnight

Cooking Time
2½-3 hours

Makes 6 servings

1 LB	yellow split peas
½ LB	salt beef, diced
8 CUPS	water
1	small turnip, diced
1	large onion, diced
2	carrots, diced
	salt and pepper to taste

Dumplings

2 CUPS	all-purpose flour
2 TSP	baking powder
½ TSP	salt
2 TBSP	butter
¾ CUP	milk

1. Soak salt beef and peas separately in water overnight.
2. Drain meat and place in large pot. Add water and bring to a boil.
3. Lower heat and simmer for 30 minutes.
4. Add peas and onion. Return to a boil, lower heat and continue to simmer for 1½ hours.
5. Add water as needed. Stir occasionally to prevent burning.
6. Add vegetables and continue to cook until tender. Stir often.
7. Add pepper to taste and salt if required.

1. In a mixing bowl combine flour, baking powder and salt.
2. Cut in butter until the mixture looks like fine crumbs.
3. Stir in milk.
4. Drop the dough into the soup, by large spoonfuls.
5. Cover (no peeking) and cook for 10 minutes.

SUGGESTED SUBSTITUTE: Many kitchens will replace the salt beef with a ham bone.

Newfoundland is home of the southernmost woodland caribou herds in the world. This young stag is from the La Poile herd and was found grazing near Rocky Ridge Pond, not far from Burgeo. In Labrador, the barren ground caribou herd is the largest such in the world with 700,000 animals.

JIGGS DINNER WITH PEASE PUDDING

	3 LBS	salt beef
	1	medium head of cabbage, cut in wedges
	5 OR 6	carrots
	3 OR 4	parsnips
	6 OR 8	potatoes, halved
	2	medium turnip, sliced
	4	small onions

Preparation Time
30 minutes

Soaking Time
Overnight

Cooking Time
3 hours

Makes 4-6 servings

Pease Pudding

1½ CUPS	dried yellow split peas

1. Soak salt beef and peas separately in water overnight.
2. Drain meat, rinse with clean water and place in a large pot. Cover with fresh water.
3. Drain peas and place in a cloth pudding bag and tie. Put bag in pot with beef. Cover pot.
4. Bring to a boil. Lower heat and simmer for 2 hours.
5. Peel and prepare vegetables.
6. Place vegetables in pot and cook until tender.

SUGGESTED SUBSTITUTE: Beef brisket makes an acceptable substitute to salt beef.

BAKED BEANS

Preparation Time
40 minutes

Soaking Time
Overnight

Baking Time
6-7 hours

Makes 6 servings

2 CUPS	dried white pea beans
2	onions, sliced
½ CUP	salt pork, diced
2 TBSP	cider vinegar
½ TSP	salt
½ CUP	light molasses
¼ CUP	ketchup
½ TSP	mustard
1 TBSP	brown sugar
	pepper to taste
	hot water as needed

1. Soak beans in cold water overnight.
2. Pour beans and water in which they were soaked into saucepan. Bring to boil and simmer for 30 minutes.
3. Preheat oven to 300°F.
4. Add all ingredients except onions to beans and stir.
5. Place onions in bottom of bean pot (or oven-proof dish with lid). Pour in bean mixture.
6. Add enough hot water to cover beans. Cover pot and bake for 6-8 hours.
7. Stir occasionally and add hot water as needed to keep beans moist.
8. Remove cover for last hour of baking.

SUGGESTED SUBSTITUTE: Bacon makes a delicious alternative to salt pork.

Lobster pots surround Mr. Norman Day, of Harbour Breton, as he readies a trawl. A trawl is 50 fathoms of main line, or 300 feet, with a half-fathom sud line evenly spaced every fathom along the main line, to which the baited hooks are secured.

An iceberg about the size of a house, rather small by iceberg standards, offers a safe refuge for this juvenile gull in St. Anthony Bight. The most common gulls in Newfoundland are the Great Black Back, Herring Gull and Black-Legged Kittiwake. The term seagull is actually a misnomer.

RAMEA-STYLE RIBS

Preparation Time
15 minutes

Parboil Time
1 hour

Baking Time
2½ hours

Makes 6 servings

3 LBS	caribou ribs
¼ LB	salt pork, diced

Sauce

1 CUP	ketchup
1	onion, diced
2 TBSP	brown sugar
1 TBSP	lemon juice
1 TSP	white vinegar
1 TBSP	mustard
1 TSP	salt
¼ TSP	pepper

1. Place ribs in large pot. Cover with water. Bring to a boil and simmer for one hour.
2. Preheat oven to 350°F.
3. Transfer ribs and ½ cup of liquid to a roasting pan. Cover ribs with salt pork and bake uncovered ½ hour or until browned.
4. In a mixing bowl combine sauce ingredients.
5. Pour over ribs and bake uncovered for 2 hours. Baste ribs often with sauce.

SUGGESTED SUBSTITUTE: Any rack of ribs, such as beef or pork, may be used instead of caribou. As a substitute to salt pork drippings, try adding two tablespoons of your favourite cooking oil.

TOM JANES RECIPE

Preparation Time	2 LBS	moose meat, cubed
15 minutes	1	10-oz can mushroom soup
Baking Time	8-OZ	ginger ale
2 hours	1	package of onion soup mix
Makes 4 servings		

1. Preheat oven to 325°F.
2. In bowl, combine meat, can soup and ginger ale.
3. Pour into casserole dish. Sprinkle onion soup mix over the mixture.
4. Cover and bake for 2 hours until meat is tender. Stir once.

SUGGESTED SUBSTITUTE: Beef or caribou can be substituted with confidence.

Few things evoke a sense of place as does an aroma lingering in the air, be it salt spray, smoke from a chimney or the crème-de-la-crème... fresh cut hay. Mr. John Manning, and daughter Tammy, of Cuslett, on the Cape Shore, harvest their hay crop the traditional way.

PLANKED ATLANTIC SALMON—BBQ STYLE

I first had planked salmon while working at a fishing lodge on the Grey River. The fish was done over an open fire in a natural rock oven and the flavour was simply exquisite. Once home, this marinade was developed by way of trial-and-error and has evolved into a summer favourite.

Preparation Time
30 minutes

Marinate Time
4-6 hours

Cooking Time
30-40 minutes

Makes 4-6 servings

1	salmon fillet, 3–4 lbs

Dill Sauce

¾ CUP	sour cream
3 TBSP	cucumber, finely chopped
2 TBSP	fresh dill, finely chopped
3 TBSP	green onions, finely chopped

Marinade

2 CUPS	water
1 CUP	brown sugar
2 CUPS	maple syrup
3 CLOVES	fresh garlic, halved
	juice from slice of fresh lemon
3 TBSP	salt
1 TSP	fresh ground black pepper
1 CUP	Jack Daniels™ bourbon

1. In large bowl combine marinade ingredients.
2. Place salmon in marinade then refrigerate for 4-6 hours.
3. In blender, combine ingredients for dill sauce and purée. Refrigerate for 4-6 hours.
4. Preheat BBQ to medium heat.
5. Brush small amount of olive oil on a plank of western red cedar. The plank should be cleaned (scrub with a bristle brush and water only) and presoaked for 24 hours in fresh water. Ensure wood has not been treated with a preservative.
6. Place planked salmon on BBQ, lower cover and cook until fish easily flakes apart with a fork. Time will depend upon thickness of plank and heat.
7. Serve with dill sauce.

DEEP-FRIED FISH OR SCALLOPS

Preparation Time
5 minutes

Cooking Time
12 minutes

Makes 4 servings

1½ LB	cod or haddock fillets or scallops
	oil (for deep-frying)
1 CUP	all-purpose flour
1 CUP	water
4 TSP	baking powder
PINCH	white pepper
1 TSP	garlic salt
½ TSP	onion powder

1. In a shallow bowl, mix flour, baking powder and spices.
2. Add water and stir until batter is smooth.
3. In a deep fryer, preheat oil to 375°F.
4. Dip fish or scallops in batter and drop into hot oil. Turn once during cooking.
5. Deep-fry until crunchy and golden brown. Drain on paper towelling.

Located just east of Corner Brook, Glover Island is surrounded by the waters of Grand Lake. This 40-kilometre-long island is one of the last strongholds of Newfoundland Pine Marten, an endangered species of weasel-like animal that numbers fewer than 300.

At one time women were the backbone of the fishery. Once the men landed the fish, women would split, salt, dry, turn and pack the fish. Here, Stella Hobbs of Bunyan's Cove, located on Clode Sound, Bonavista Bay, dries squid that is destined for the Japanese market.

FISH AND BREWIS

4	**cakes of hardtack (hard bread)**
2 LBS	**salt cod bits**
1 CUP	**salt pork, diced**

Preparation Time
20 minutes

Soaking Time
Overnight

Cooking Time
20 minutes

Makes 6 servings

1. Break each cake of hardtack into 3 or 4 pieces. Soak overnight immersed in cold water.
2. In a separate bowl, soak salt cod overnight.
3. In the morning change water on the fish and lightly boil for 10 minutes. Drain.
4. In a separate saucepan, cover hardtack with water and heat until it starts to boil. Drain.
5. Mix the fish and hardtack (brewis) together in a serving dish and keep warm.
6. Fry salt pork until golden brown and crisp (scruncheons).
7. Pour scruncheons and fat over fish and brewis mixture. Serve hot.

FISH CAKES

Preparation Time
20 minutes

Soaking Time
Overnight

Cooking Time
8-10 minutes

Makes 4-6 servings

2 CUPS (1 LB)	salt cod
¼ LB	salt pork, diced
2	small onions, diced
6-8	potatoes
1 TBSP	butter
	pepper to taste
½ TSP	savoury
1	egg, beaten

1. Place cod in a bowl. Cover with water and let stand overnight. Drain and rinse.
2. Place cod in large saucepan. Cover with water and boil for 10 minutes. Drain.
3. Boil potatoes until soft. Drain.
4. Add fish, onions and savoury. Mix well. Stir in beaten egg.
5. Chill until cool and form into 3-inch patties.
6. In a skillet, sauté salt pork (scruncheons) until crisp.
7. Remove scruncheons and fry fish cakes until crisp and brown.

SUGGESTED SUBSTITUTE: If salt cod is unavailable try adding one teaspoon of salt to any white-fleshed fish and omit the overnight soaking. Vegetable oil may be used as an alternative to pork drippings.

Found on the southwest corner of the island, the Codroy Valley is one of the most important agricultural regions in the province, and arguably one of the most scenic areas too. The flat-topped Long Range Mountains, once connected to Africa, stand guard in the background.

A favourite spot of anglers and nature lovers alike is Big Falls, located on the mighty Humber River and found in Sir Richard Squires Memorial Provincial Park. During July and August it is possible to watch Atlantic Salmon leap their way over the three-metre-high falls.

FISH STEW

Preparation Time
30 minutes

Baking Time
30 minutes

Makes 4-6 servings

3 LBS	cod fillets
¼ LB	salt pork, diced
1	medium onion, sliced
5	large potatoes, sliced (¼ inch thick)
¾ CUP	boiling water
1 TSP	salt
½ TSP	pepper

1. Preheat oven to 350°F.
2. Cut fish fillets into pieces, about 2″ x 3″.
3. Place salt pork in an ovenproof dish and fry until crisp.
4. Add fish, onions and potatoes. Sprinkle with salt and pepper.
5. Pour boiling water over ingredients. Cover and place in oven.
6. Bake for 30 minutes or until potatoes are tender. Stir once during cooking and add water as needed.

SUGGESTED SUBSTITUTE: Any white-fleshed fish may be substituted for the cod. A favourite cooking oil can be a suitable substitute for pork drippings.

LOBSTER AND POTATO SALAD

Lobster
Preparation Time
20 minutes

Cooking Time
24-28 minutes

Makes 4 servings

Potato Salad
Preparation Time
20 minutes

Cooking Time
20 minutes

Makes 4 servings

4	live lobsters (1½ to 2 LBS each)
⅛ CUP	salt per quart of water

1. Fill a large cooking pot with enough water to cover lobsters. Add salt and bring water to a boil.
2. Remove rubber claw bands and place each lobster into the pot, head first. Cover and return to a boil.
3. Reduce heat and tip cover so steam can escape. Lightly boil for 20 minutes for one-pound lobster, and a further 4 minutes for each additional half-pound, until lobster turns bright red.
4. Remove from pot and allow to cool by laying the lobsters on their backs.

Potato Salad

5-7	large potatoes
2	eggs, hardboiled, sliced
½-¾ CUP	mayonnaise

1. Peel and dice potatoes.
2. Cook in lightly salted water until tender. Drain and mash.
3. In a large bowl combine potatoes and mayonnaise. Stir well.
4. Add other ingredients, as desired, except eggs. Stir well.
5. Add eggs and lightly fold in. Sprinkle top with paprika (optional).

OPTIONAL INGREDIENTS FOR POTATO SALAD: Finely chopped or diced small onion, celery, ham, green onions or green peppers.

Truly one of the important cultural towns in the province would have to be Trinity. Founded by the Portuguese on Trinity Day, 1501, the town can lay claim to holding the first court of justice in the New World, in 1610. It was also here that Dr. John Clinch administered the first smallpox vaccine in North America.

On the shores of Trinity Bay, Mr. & Mrs. Bernard Sooley prepare a fresh catch of cod at their Heart's Delight stage. The larger cod will be filleted, while the smaller fish—called rounders—are split and lightly pickled in salt brine to produce what is known as corned fish.

COD AU GRATIN

Preparation Time
20 minutes

Baking Time
30 minutes

Makes 4 servings

1 LB	cod, cut into cubes
1	small onion, diced
1½ CUPS	white sauce

White Sauce

¼ CUP	butter
¼ CUP	all-purpose flour
½ TSP	salt
⅛ TSP	pepper
1¼ CUPS	milk

Topping

½ CUP	fine breadcrumbs
2 TBSP	butter
1 TSP	salt
	pepper to taste
½ CUP	grated cheddar cheese

1. In saucepan, melt butter for white sauce.
2. Blend in flour, salt and pepper. Heat and stir until bubbly.
3. Gradually add the milk, stirring until smooth.
4. Bring to boil. Cook and stir for 1 to 2 minutes longer.
5. Preheat oven to 375°F.
6. Place cubed cod in greased baking dish. Add onion to white sauce and pour sauce over fish.
7. Microwave butter for topping until melted. Stir in breadcrumbs.
8. Sprinkle breadcrumb mixture over sauce and top with grated cheese.
9. Bake for 30 minutes.

SUGGESTED SUBSTITUTE: With minimal change in flavour, any white-fleshed fish may be used.

SALT FISH AND PORK SCRAPS

Preparation Time
15 minutes

Soaking Time
Overnight

Cooking Time
25 minutes

Makes 4 servings

1 LB	salt fish bits
¼ LB	salt pork, diced

1. Soak fish in cold water overnight.
2. Change water and boil fish for 15 minutes. Drain.
3. In large skillet fry pork scraps until browned.
4. Add drained fish and fry for additional 10 minutes.
5. Serve with boiled potatoes.

The Atlantic Puffin is the official bird of Newfoundland and Labrador. Underwater the bird uses its short, strong wings for propulsion and its feet as rudders. There are about 365,000 breeding pairs in North America ranging from Maine to the Arctic; about 60% of these breed in Witless Bay.

Labrador, as seen along the distant shoreline, is separated from the mainland portion of the province by the Strait of Belle Isle. Between 1520 and 1600, Basque whalers from France and Spain enjoyed a thriving and lucrative whaling industry in these waters.

SCALLOP CASSEROLE

Preparation Time
20 minutes

Baking Time
35-40 minutes

Makes 2 servings

½ LB	scallops, diced or halved
½ LB	mushrooms, sliced
1	medium onion, finely chopped
2 TBSP	butter
1 CUP	buttered breadcrumbs
1 CUP	grated cheese (mozzarella or cheddar)

White Sauce

2 TBSP	butter
2 TBSP	all-purpose flour
½ TSP	salt
PINCH	pepper
1 CUP	milk

1. In saucepan, melt butter for white sauce.
2. Blend in flour, salt, and pepper. Heat and stir until bubbly.
3. Gradually add the milk, stirring until smooth.
4. Bring to a boil. Cook 1 to 2 minutes longer, stirring constantly.
5. Preheat oven to 350°F.
6. Sauté onion and mushrooms in butter for 10 minutes.
7. Add with scallops to the white sauce. Stir.
8. Pour into casserole dish. Sprinkle with breadcrumbs and cheese.
9. Bake for 35 to 40 minutes.

Preparation Time
20 minutes

Baking Time
2 hours

Makes 6 servings

3 CUPS	stale bread, cubed
¼ CUP	butter, melted
½ CUP	brown sugar
3 TBSP	molasses
½ CUP	raisins
1 TSP	baking soda
1 TBSP	hot water
½ CUP	all-purpose flour
1 TSP	ginger
1 TSP	allspice
1 TSP	cinnamon
PINCH	salt

Sweet Sauce

½ CUP	cup butter
1 CUP	icing sugar
1	egg, beaten
½ TSP	vanilla

1. Heat water in bottom half of a double boiler.
2. In top half, cream butter then blend in sugar and egg.
3. Place over hot water. Beat constantly with a whisk until foamy.
4. Add vanilla. Stir. Serve hot over figgy duff.

1. Soak bread in water for a few minutes. Squeeze out water.
2. In a large bowl, mix together bread, butter, brown sugar, molasses and raisins.
3. Combine baking soda and water. Add to mixture and stir.
4. Combine flour and spices. Add to mixture and stir well.
5. Pour into a greased pudding mold. Cover with aluminum foil.
6. Place mold in a steamer or large pot and add boiling water. Cover and steam for 2 hours or until firm to the touch (*pudding mixture can also be placed in a pudding bag and boiled with Jiggs Dinner for 2 hours*).
7. Top with sweet sauce.

FIGGY DUFF

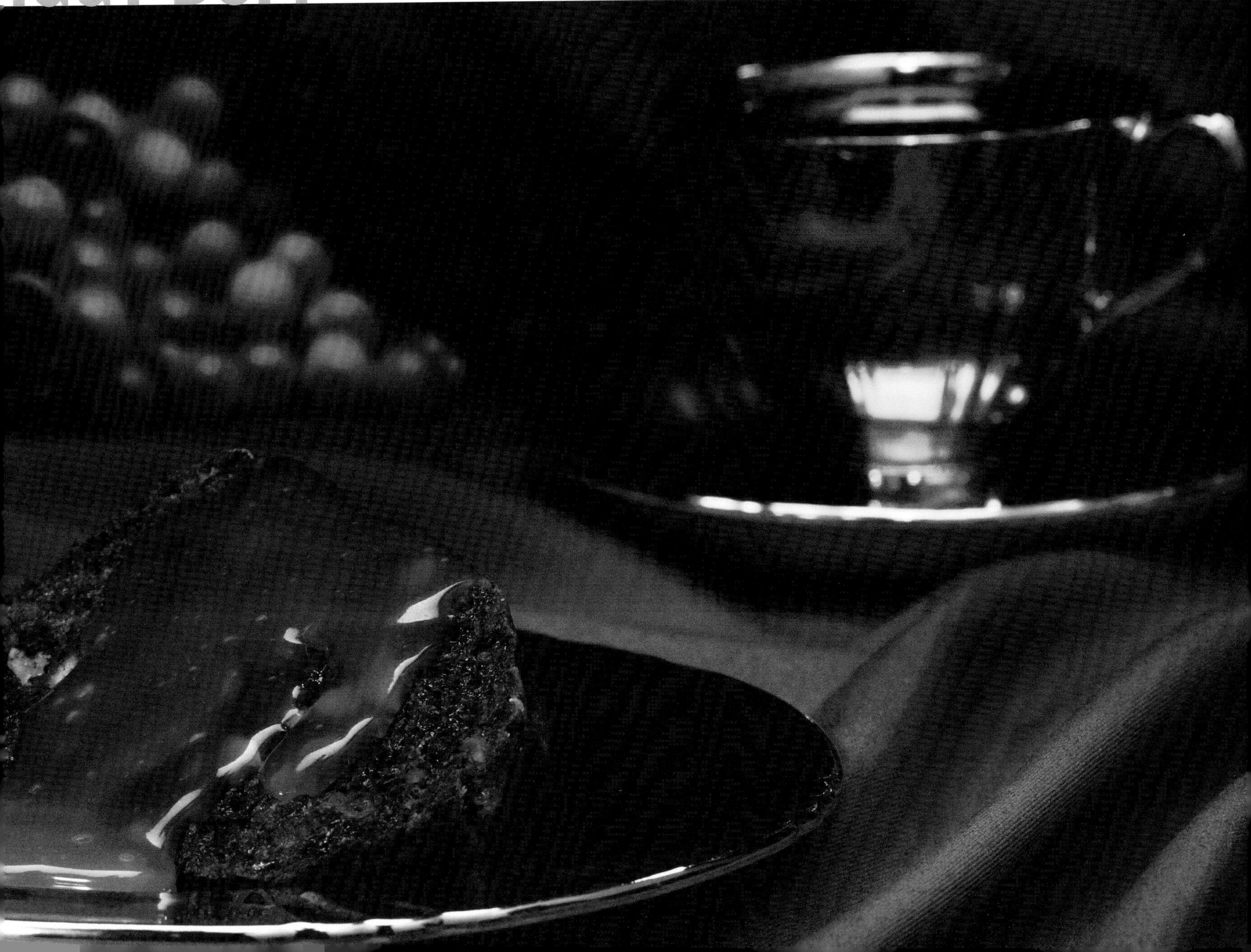

Located just 45 kilometres from the ferry terminus at Port aux Basques, Rose Blanche is one of the first communities many visitors to the province will see. The lighthouse, built in 1873 and restored in 1999, is the only working granite lighthouse in Canada.

BREAD PUDDING

Preparation Time
20 minutes

Baking Time
1 hour

Makes 6 servings

2 CUPS	stale bread, cubed
½ CUP	granulated sugar
¼ CUP	raisins
¼ CUP	flaked coconut (optional)
2	eggs, beaten
1½ CUPS	milk
1 TSP	vanilla

1. Preheat oven to 375°F.
2. Mix all ingredients and pour into greased casserole dish.
3. Stand dish in pan of water. Bake for 1 hour.
4. Top with brown sugar sauce.

Brown Sugar Sauce

2 TBSP	butter
½ CUP	lightly packed brown sugar
2 TBSP	all-purpose flour
¼ TSP	salt
1 CUP	water
½ TSP	vanilla

1. In a saucepan melt butter. Blend in brown sugar, flour and salt.
2. Gradually stir in water and cook, stirring constantly until thickened.
3. Remove from heat and blend in vanilla.

BLUEBERRIES AND DOUGHBOYS

Preparation Time
20 minutes

Cooking Time
30 minutes

Makes 6 servings

¾ CUP	granulated sugar
½ CUP	water
4 CUPS	blueberries

1. In a large saucepan, boil sugar and water for 5 minutes.
2. Add berries and continue to boil until soft.

Doughboys

2 CUPS	all-purpose flour
3 TSP	baking powder
½ TSP	salt
1 TBSP	granulated sugar
1 TBSP	butter
⅔ CUP	milk

1. Sift dry ingredients together. Cut in butter.
2. Pour milk into mixture and stir.
3. Divide into 6 portions and drop from a spoon into boiling blueberries.
4. Cover and cook rapidly for 15 minutes (no peeking).
5. Place doughboys in individual serving dish. Cover with boiled blueberries and top with whipped cream.

The old Cape Spear Lighthouse is the second oldest in the province, and served as a beacon for St. John's Harbour from 1836 until 1955, when the new concrete lighthouse was constructed. St. John's first navigational light was located at Fort Amherst and was built in 1813.

Located on the south side of Bonne Bay are the 600-metre-high Tablelands. The peridotite rock that forms this plateau was thrust upward by way of plate tectonics and was at one time the earth's upper mantle. This rock is so rich in magnesium and iron that it supports very little plant life.

PINEAPPLE SQUARES

Preparation Time
20 minutes

Baking Time
35 minutes

Makes 24 squares

¾ CUP	butter
¼ CUP	granulated sugar
1½ CUPS	all-purpose flour
¼ TSP	salt
1	19-oz can crushed pineapple, drained
1	egg
¾ CUP	lightly packed brown sugar
¼ TSP	salt
½ TSP	vanilla
½ CUP	flaked coconut

1. Preheat oven to 325°F.
2. Cream together butter and granulated sugar.
3. Blend in flour and salt.
4. Press into a 9-inch square baking pan.
5. Pour drained pineapple over base and spread.
6. Beat together egg, brown sugar, salt, vanilla and coconut.
7. Spread evenly over pineapple.
8. Bake for 35 minutes until golden brown.

Within earshot of bustling downtown St. John's, the Battery maintains its centuries-old charm, and welcomes mariners as they pass through the Narrows and into the sheltered harbour. The Battery was so named because of the guns that were emplaced here in 1673 to fight off pirates.

Lar's Fruit Mart, in downtown St. John's, is a landmark in the capitol city and has been standing guard here for more than 50 years. In stark contrast the area has given way to the bustle of boulevard traffic, overhead pedways, glass office towers, convention centres and Mile One Stadium.

ACKNOWLEDGEMENTS

At the end of the day I came to the realization that creating this book was more than capturing images, editing the recipe selections and writing the captions. It had become a sanctuary of reflection: of sounds and smells that had tantalized my senses in the past; of stories told on the end of a stage, of walks down George Street in St. John's and of shredded socks—with an axe—in Lobstick, Labrador in -42°F temperatures.

More accurately, however, this book is about people and this project would not have been without the support and encouragement of the publisher, Mr. Garry Cranford, who approached my work with such enthusiasm and confidence.

It was his suggestion that I assemble the team I wanted to work with on this project. And what a team it was: from food stylist, designers, printer, editors and support staff, each one of these professionals epitomizes the very meaning of the word. In no particular order many thanks to Debbie Arthurs Page, Jan Sykora, Tom Klassen and Jacques Thibault. It has truly been a pleasure to work with each one of you.

Although many of the recipes in this book are traditional and their origin unknown, each was tested in our home kitchen. Not only is Julie my life's partner, she was also instrumental on this project. It was she who did the brunt of the support work: from locating the recipes, to testing, and then collecting and re-writing them. Thanks, Julie, but you never did tell me what a half-eggshell of sugar translated to?

And to all those in this great province who have shared their stories and tables with me during my travels—Thank You.